Power Prayers

21 DAY DEVOTIONAL
& PRAYER JOURNEY

Christina Moseley-Rolle

Book Publishing Consultant: Dr. Lorneka Joseph – drlorneka.co

Editing: Dr. Brenda Randle – thewritingdr.com

Cover Design and Formatting: Ya Ya Ya Creative – yayayacreative.com

ISBN 978-1-7363430-0-5

PRINTED AND BOUND IN THE UNITED STATES OF AMERICA

Dedication

First, I would like to dedicate this book to my husband, Nathan Rolle. Thank you for your support, love and believing in me. You've encouraged me to keep pushing when I didn't have the energy to do so. I love you. You were the one to prophesy to me that I would write a #1 Best Seller.

To my wonderful children Alyanna, Abigail and Devon, you are my rays of sunshine as I arise each morning. You give me hope to be the best mother and role model you need me to be. I love you all dearly.

To my parents Rudolph and Patricia "Delly" Moseley and my siblings Lovern, Rudy, Ryan and Lorenzo, you are the wind beneath my wings. Mom and Dad, without you, there would be no me. My siblings, you are all my bouncing pads; you keep me grounded in the face of adversity. I love each of you.

To Apostle Gail McKinney-Johnson, the lady who took me under her wing 5 years ago. She taught me how to pray and the importance of prayer in a believer's life while awakening the intercessor in me. Thank you for mentoring me when I came to you and said, "God sent me to you to teach me for a season." You are not just my mentor; you are also a friend.

To Mrs. Candice Turnquest, my personal development coach and friend. There is a time and season for everything under the sun. We connected in 2019, I knew then that God had more for me. You helped bring my life into perspective with your Christ-like love and truth. Thank you.

To my church family, thank you for allowing me to be the First Lady God needed me to be for each of you. I love you all.

Finally, to two amazing ladies, my publishing coach Dr. Lorneka Joseph and editor Dr. Brenda Randle. Thank you both for taking the assignment. Thank you for your guidance, honesty and cutting-edge work. You've always encouraged me and were always there to answer any questions. You kept me calm when I believed it wasn't possible. Thank you for the investment.

Preface

Prayer and God's word are essential parts of a believer's life. These things connect the individual to a being higher than themselves. Many times, individuals feel and know they have the answers or solutions to whatever concerns them in their personal life. When I decided to write this devotional, I began writing from the position of a mother, a wife and the many hats I wear daily. I saw the areas that were most troubling and burdening. I thought about the areas I was most broken in and the areas that needed rebuilding. As a pastor's wife, I felt a tugging in my heart for the women in the congregation that also struggled with the idea of prayer and God's word. I knew they had concerns related to how to connect and effectively pray for the areas that mattered to them. God spoke to me clearly on July 15, 2019 with the following message: "Gather the ladies in the church, a few of my prayer partners and two close friends to journey with me as I consecrated." For 21 days, we would devote 5 minutes of our day to sing, pray, meditate on a passage of scripture and allow God to reveal Himself as our help. I allowed them to share (as they felt led) on areas they wanted us to cover in prayer.

At the time, I didn't know the magnitude and the purpose of this journey; I was being obedient to the voice of God. The number

"21" came to me as I remembered the story of Daniel. In Daniel chapter 10, Daniel fasted and prayed for 21 days (3 weeks) after which he received answers and direction to his request. Daniel 10:12 (NKJV) states, "Then he said to me, "Do not fear, Daniel, for from the first day that you set your heart to understand, and to humble yourself before your God, your words were heard; and I have come because of your words." I felt confident in this verse that signs, power, deliverance and breakthrough happen in praying and devoting time to God for 21 days. I felt this way because the angel of the Lord (meaning messenger) came to Daniel to deliver a word in the same way.

Each daily devotional topic was a surprise. I never knew what areas God would want me to focus on until the night before I went to sleep. As I lay my head on the bed, I would hear His voice tell me "tomorrow this is what I want you to focus and pray on." Every morning I would rise and feel the presence of God strong in my prayer space as I studied the scripture topic and began writing with my pen. The thoughts would flow smoothly and divinely. As the days passed, the ladies would each say how this daily devotional was a tool and a building block for their walk with God. We had mothers testifying about victory from court cases as they journeyed for the 21 days.

Prayer and the word are your weapons of mass destruction against the powers of darkness. I believe that as you commit yourself to God for the next 21 days, you will receive direction and empowerment. You will draw closer to God and He to you. You will hear his voice clearer as He speaks. Your assigned angel will come to you and declare thus says the Lord. The Lord will show you the vision of what is to come. Embrace your next level and dimension in prayer. You have been waiting on answers to your problems and situations of life. Today, God is your help and He has His hand stretched down to meet your hand. Will you hold it and take this journey with Him? I guarantee you will end feeling tremendously blessed, becoming more spiritually enriched by the move of God.

Table of Contents

Introduction

The Lord himself goes before you and will be with you;
He will never leave you nor forsake you.
Do not be afraid; do not be discouraged.

–DEUTERONOMY 31:8

O ften times in life, we wonder, "Why me?" What did I do to deserve this? Is this really happening to me? It seems like God doesn't love me anymore. But through it all, God loves you and He cares for you. He has a plan and a purpose for your life. It is nothing you have done that caused things to happen to you or make your life the way it is. One thing is for sure, it does not have to be that way if you begin to see God as your divine helper in every area of your life and in every situation you face.

Do you know spending time with God through reading, meditating, praying and speaking positive, can change the outcome of any situation? If you want to see your life change; you need to spend time with God daily and speak to your environment. The things that are out of alignment will begin to align themselves with the purpose and plan God has for your life. God has a purpose and a plan for your life. You need to position yourself; meaning position your **MINDSET**, to see what God has in store for you.

God shaped the world by speaking light into darkness. He spoke life to a dying situation and death was cursed and disappeared. We, as His children, have that same power. It is time for us to exercise our power on earth. The word of God says to speak those things that are not as though they were. Declare it, and it shall be established. Ask, and it shall be given unto you.

The focus of this devotional book is to allow God to reveal Himself as your help in areas which are near and dear to your heart. Also, commit time to God in prayer and reading of His word. As you journey with God, He is about to bring your life, and everything pertaining to your life, in order in the next 21 days. Your life is going to start making sense. You will not be confused any longer. You will begin to see and operate your life with order because you will trust God completely.

The number 21 is a unique number. It represents divine angelic assistance and breakthrough.

- Number 2 is known as the number of relationships, cooperation, diplomacy and trust

- Number 1 usually represents new beginnings and positive attitude.

- ❈ 7 (Perfection) x 3 (Resurrection) =21 – God is about to resurrect and perfect things in your life that concern you

- ❈ Daniel prayed and fasted for 21 days and received help and an answer from God through the angel. Daniel 10: 10-12

For the next 21 days, begin with the following:

- ❈ Praying the prayer of change; followed by

- ❈ The devotional for each day.

I guarantee you will begin to see your environment change and have a new perspective on life.

Prayer of Commitment
TO BEGIN THE 21 DAY JOURNEY

Lord,

I commit myself to You. I desire to be a vessel You can use. I know that You have great plans for me and it only comes through knowing and spending time with You. I realize that what I may think, You think greater and deeper for me. You want to use me greatly. I just have to commit and stay focused. So, Lord, here I am. I submit my mind, body, and spirit to You. I thank You in advance for the new beginning in my life.

Amen.

Day 1 GOD, MY HELP WITH TROUBLE

God is our refuge and strength, a very present help in trouble.

–PSALM 46:1

Devotion

God is our present help in times of trouble means God is here to help at any time we need Him. He is with us every second, minute, hour, day, month and year; especially in times of trouble. Trouble could be anything that brings pain, anxiety, grief, disaster, frustration, disappointment, misunderstanding, loss, or anger. Whatever your trouble may be, God says today when trouble comes, do not fear because I am your help. What is it that you need help with today? God is saying, I am your refuge. I will cover you. I have your back. I am your strength. I will give you the wisdom you need to face your trouble; just rest in me. I am present at this moment to lead and guide you into all truth.

Let Us Pray

Our Heavenly Father;

Come in the midst of us today and help us. Give us the wisdom, the knowledge, and the understanding that we need in our troubling situation. We lay it at your feet. We thank you for your peace that is keeping us. In Jesus name, we pray.

Amen.

REFLECTION

REFLECTION

Day 2

GOD, MY HELP WITH FEAR

So we may boldly say, "The Lord is my helper; I will not fear. What can man do to me?"

–HEBREWS 13:6

Devotion

In today's scripture, we read that God is our helper in times of fear. What is fear? It is a feeling, an unpleasant emotion caused by the threat of danger, pain, or harm. What or who has you fearful today? Is it fear of losing the job, the relationship, the friendship, the car? Is it fear of the doctor's report or the child that maybe on the wrong path or taking care of retired parents? What is the fear or who is the fear? Do you know God has not given us the spirit of fear but of power, love, and a sound mind? He is our helper to cast off that emotion. It is just a feeling. We are children of faith not doubt. God is saying, I am here to help. Put the fear on Me. I am here to assist you, to partner with you, to gird you up. Don't allow your thoughts to be flooded. Cast your cares on Me because I care.

I encourage you today to lay your fears on the altar of Christ. He can and will work it out.

Let Us Pray

Our Heavenly Father;

Today, I need You to comfort me in my time of fear. I believe and trust in Your word. No weapon formed against me will prosper. I'm in the palm of Your hand today. In Jesus name, I pray.

Amen.

REFLECTION

REFLECTION

_____

_____

_____

_____

_____

_____

_____

_____

_____

_____

_____

_____

_____

_____

_____

_____

_____

Day 3 GOD, MY HELP WITH PARENTING

Train up a child in the way he should go,
and when he is old he will not depart from it.

–PROVERBS 22:6

Devotion

Parenting is a difficult task. We know our children can do things, and say things that cause us pain. But God, who is our helper, teaches us in all things to be prayerful. He says in James 1: 5, "If any of you lacks wisdom, let him ask of God, who gives to all liberally and without reproach, and it will be given to him." Today, we need God to help us in raising godly children; to raise them to become productive citizens in society, loving husbands, and supportive wives who are saved, love Jesus and on fire for God. The scripture shows us in Jeremiah 31: 15-17 where children will stray from the Lord; away from the teachings that you as their parent taught them according to Proverbs 22: 6. There is comfort today! God reminds us that he is here to deliver. He gives us this promise in Isaiah 54: 13, "All your children shall be taught by the Lord, and great shall be the peace of your children." How wonderful are these words today! How comforting are these words from our Heavenly Father. I declare over your child Isaiah 49: 25, the Lord will save your child.

Let Us Pray

Our Heavenly Father;

Thank You for the hope You give me today. As You give me the wisdom in how to raise my children, they will become all You have created them to be. In Jesus name, I pray.

Amen.

REFLECTION

_____

_____

_____

_____

_____

_____

_____

_____

_____

_____

_____

_____

_____

_____

_____

_____

_____

REFLECTION

_____

_____

_____

_____

_____

_____

_____

_____

_____

_____

_____

_____

_____

_____

Day 4

GOD, MY HELP WITH SELF CONTROL

*Whoever has no rule over his own spirit
is like a city broken down, without walls.*

–PROVERBS 25:28

Devotion

Self-Control is defined as the ability to regulate one's emotions, thoughts, and behavior in the face of temptations and impulses. The Bible admonishes us in Galatians 5: 23 to have self-control which is a principal that guides a Christian's conduct. What is it today, or should I say, what area in your life are you not exercising self-control? Is it impulsive buying, impulsive spending, lying, unforgiveness, sexual promiscuity, lust, gluttony, fornication, emotionally abusing yourself with negative thoughts, eating disorder, unproductiveness, over cleaning? Whatever it is, call it out and know today that God is here to help you conquer this area where you lack self-control and gain victory over it. Lack of self-control causes an individual to do, say, and respond in a way that more often brings about a negative reaction and result. Proverbs

25: 28 (English Standard Version) says, "A man without self-control is like a city broken into and left without walls." Psalms 121 is perfect to pray in times like these to repent from sin, ask God to come into your heart, and to take complete control. We need self-control because the enemy is seeking any uncontrolled soul to devour. Let us clothe ourselves in the armor of God, clothe our thoughts, and submit our bodies to the Lordship of Christ today.

Let Us Pray

Our Heavenly Father;

I commit my life, my thoughts, and my actions to You today. Help me to maintain self-control in the areas of my life where I struggle. Preserve me in my going out and coming in. Don't allow me to slip and fall back. You are my help. In Jesus name, I pray.

Amen.

REFLECTION

_____

_____

_____

_____

_____

_____

_____

_____

_____

_____

_____

_____

_____

_____

_____

_____

REFLECTION

Day 5

GOD, MY HELP WITH WORK

Then God blessed them, and God said to them,
"Be fruitful and multiply; fill the earth and subdue it:
have dominion over the fish of the sea, over the birds of the air,
and over every living thing that moves on the earth."

–GENESIS 1:28

And whatever you do, do it heartily, as to the Lord and not to men.

–COLOSSIANS 3:23-25

Devotion

Happy is the person who finds joy in their work. How do you find joy with work? The first thing is to acknowledge that God is the divine creator of work. In Genesis 1: 28, we read that God gave man dominion in the Garden of Eden to take care of it, to rule over it, to keep it in order. Where has God placed you? Am I taking care of where God has me? Am I keeping order? Am I a good leader with my job duties and responsibilities? How is my working relationship with my coworkers and my supervisor? Is it favorable or strained? What about if you are the supervisor? How are your leadership skills? How are your human skills with your employees and your cognitive skills (your ability to solve day to day problems)? Can we truly say, we are working as unto the Lord? If so, good, and you will receive your just reward. If you have a question mark, then you have work to do.

Let's examine our work ethic and allow God to be our helper. In Colossians 3: 23-25, we read, "And whatever you do, do it heartily as to the Lord and not to men, knowing that from the Lord you will receive the reward of the inheritance; for you serve the Lord Christ. But he who does wrong will be repaid for what he has done, and there is no partiality." Before this scripture can become alive in us, we need to ensure that God has placed us in the right garden. Where is your work garden? Is this where God wants you to work heartily? The problem, or should I say a challenge, we face is sometimes we may be in the wrong Garden. Because of the responsibilities we have presently, we have to work in this environment until the dream job comes along. This is understandable. If this is the case, I encourage you to daily acknowledge God in all your ways that He will direct your path. Direct your path on how giving you favor with your supervisor, customers, and employees until He opens the door for you to move to the garden prepared for you. No use complaining, becoming angry, and bitter because you will only make matters worse and lack the fruit of the spirit and work productively. If you are in your right work garden but having trouble working heartily, meditate on Proverbs 3. God outlines the importance of gaining wisdom and understanding from Him on how to maneuver with work and work relationships. He is our help today. Wisdom is our guiding light.

Let Us Pray

Our Heavenly Father;

I acknowledge that You know what is best for me and my work life. Lead me to the place where I am bringing You glory and honor with my thoughts, words and actions at work. I desire to please You in all that I do. In Jesus name, I pray.

Amen.

REFLECTION

REFLECTION

Day 6 GOD, MY HELP WITH CONFUSION

For God is not the author of confusion, but of peace.

–1 CORINTHIANS 14:33

Devotion

Confusion is defined as uncertainty about what is happening, intended, or required. It is to be unclear in one's mind about something. Did you know when you are confused, it is difficult to hear and understand God's instructions? Our lives encompass so many layers. Whether it is marriage, children, our jobs, grandkids, friendships, relationships, ministry, taking care of parents, family, or career often times produces situations that bring about a level of confusion. It is bound to happen! In those situations, those confusing situations, what do you do? Do you respond in anger, in fear, in disbelief, or even in silence which could be a bit of rebellion? In the story in Mark 4: 35-41 (Jesus and the disciples in the boat), we see how the disciples were faced with a situation that was not familiar to them. They instantly became confused, which produced a level of fear in them. Jesus, after calming the waves and the storm, asked them a question, "Why are you so fearful? How is it that you have no faith?" Jesus knew a storm was coming but He was sleeping because He knew that the storm would not harm them. God is not the author of confusion according to 1 Corinthians 14: 33. His presence will not manifest in a confusing environment; the enemy manifest in a confusing environment. What did Jesus do when confusion arose?

1. He arose (acted in the authority of who He was - the son of God)

2. He rebuked the wind (the contrary spirit that was trying to breathe and hover over them) which brought the confusing spirit

3. He spoke the word of God (peace be still)

James 4: 7 says, "Therefore submit to God, resist the devil and he will flee from you." Jesus displayed this verse in full action in this situation. Today, God is our helper. He left for us a comforter and teacher to help us. This is the Holy Spirit. The Holy Spirit is our helper. He gives us the knowledge, the understanding, and wisdom in all things. Let us activate the Holy Spirit in our lives. Ask him to reside in your heart today and show you the way to go. When you are faced with a confusing spirit, remember to:

1. Stand in your authority (you are a child of the King, call on His name to fight on your behalf)

2. Rebuke the confusing spirit. Let the mind of Christ be your mind. God has not given you the spirit of fear, but of power, love, and a sound mind

3. Speak the word. The Holy Spirit will bring to your remembrance the word. Make sure you study and meditate on God's word. God can only help those who help themselves

Let Us Pray

Our Heavenly Father;

I renounce any thoughts that cloud my judgment. I stand boldly in my authority as a child of the King that peace reigns in my situation because You are not the author of confusion. Your presence is now amidst my situation. In Jesus name, I pray.

Amen.

REFLECTION

_____

_____

_____

_____

_____

_____

_____

_____

_____

_____

_____

_____

_____

_____

_____

REFLECTION

Day 7 GOD, MY HELP WITH WELLNESS

Or do you not know that your body is the temple of the Holy Spirit
who is in you, whom you have from God, and you are not your own?
–1 CORINTHIANS 6:19-20

Supplemental References:
1 CORINTHIANS 6:12, ECCLESIASTES 3:13, 1 CORINTHIANS 10:13.
PROVERBS 25:27, and 1 CORINTHIANS 10:31

Devotion

Do you know God desires you to have a healthy lifestyle? Our bodies belong to God. We were created in His image and in His likeness to bring glory to His name. We all have a purpose on this earth and God wants us to be healthy to fulfill the promises He has given to us and spoken over our lives. We have to know that food is for our benefit according to Genesis 9: 3, "Every moving thing that lives shall be food for you. And as I gave you the green plants, I give you everything." Food is our fuel to function from day to day. The problem comes in when we make poor health choices daily which we will eventually pay for later with sickness and diseases.

God is not saying ice cream is bad or the salt and vinegar potato chip is bad, neither is the meat lovers' pizza washed down with a cold icy Coca-Cola™. What is bad and unhealthy is having this in lack of moderation. There is a time and place for everything under the sun. Today, if you struggle with unhealthy eating, God is here to help. Ask Him to transform your mind and renew it. To help you to think on what is good and lovely. To enjoy your food and not see it as a punishment because food is a gift of God. It is how you manage it. If you are tempted to make healthy choices, God promised in 1 Corinthians 10: 13, "No temptation has overtaken you except such as is common to man; but God is faithful, who will not allow you to be tempted beyond that you are able, but with the temptation will also make the way of escape, that you may be able to bear it." As you go about your day remember, whatever you do, do all to the glory of God.

Let Us Pray

Our Heavenly Father;

I thank You today that You are teaching me how to make healthy choices. This body is Your body and from this day forth I will not defile it. I will nurture it to bring glory and honor to Your name. In Jesus name, I pray.

Amen.

REFLECTION

_____

_____

_____

_____

_____

_____

_____

_____

_____

_____

_____

_____

_____

_____

_____

REFLECTION

_____

_____

_____

_____

_____

_____

_____

_____

_____

_____

_____

_____

_____

_____

_____

_____

_____

Day 8
GOD, MY HELP WITH FRIENDSHIPS

A friend loves at all times, and a brother is born for adversity.
–PROVERBS 17:17

Supplemental References:
PROVERBS 12:36, PROVERBS 19:21, and 1 CORINTHIANS 15:33

Devotion

God is a relational God. Everything He created He thought about the relationship to each other or how what He created could benefit others. From the beginning of time, this was taking place. Relationships are important to God. They should be important to you also. Take a roll call of your friendships in your circle. Ask yourself these questions;

1. My friends are genuinely happy for me when I share good news

2. I can always count on my friends to cover me in prayer without thinking they have an alternative motive

3. My friends are truthful to me

4. I can share my goals, private thoughts, and not here it again from another person

5. My friend weeps with me during sad times

6. My friend brings out the best in me

7. My friend encourages me to pursue my dreams

8. My friend is loyal

9. My friend provides wise counsel even though I don't want to hear it sometimes

10. My friend loves me till the end never judging

Friendship is defined as a state of mutual trust and support. It is a relationship between people who are always there for each other. As people of God, we should be very concerned about who we choose as friends. Friends are there to help in times of need. A true friend should give more than they receive from you. 1 Corinthians 15: 33 encourages us to be careful not to be misled because bad company corrupts good character. A true friend is handpicked by God and will always lead you in the right direction. I encourage you to examine your heart. Ask the Lord to help you discern who should be your friends and who does not need to be your friend. If there is someone in your life that is a bad influence, ask the Lord to help you to cut them out - to remove them from your space. Don't feel bad when individuals walk out of your life or get mad when you cut them out. You are commanded in Proverbs 12: 26 to choose your friends carefully because the way of the wicked leads you astray. Trust the Lord that he knows what is best for you. Remember these parting words from Proverbs 19: 21, "There are many plans in a man's heart, nevertheless the Lord's counsel - that will stand." Today, let us pray about all the areas of friendship that concern us, work, church, the opposite sex, social friendships, and school.

Let Us Pray

Our Heavenly Father;

Thank You for the gift of friendship. I ask that You will connect me with the right friends in this season and remove individuals that will not benefit my life. In Jesus name, I pray.

Amen.

REFLECTION

REFLECTION

Day 9

GOD, MY HELP WITH THOUGHTS

For as he thinks in his heart, so is he.

–PROVERBS 23:7

For I know the thoughts that I think toward you says the Lord,
thoughts of peace and not of evil, to give you a future and a hope.

–JEREMIAH 29:11

Devotion

The mind is the battle field. The way we think about life, about ourselves, about the things that concern us on a daily basis will manifest in our lives either in a positive or negative way. As righteous people of God who hold up the blood stain banner, we should always think positive in good and bad situations. Thinking negative all the time can make you sick, make you angry, bitter, restless, eventually turning your heart cold. God's promise of help is found in Jeremiah 29: 11 which says "For I know the thoughts that I think toward you says the Lord, thoughts of peace and not of evil, to give you a future and a hope." Wow! What powerful, comforting, and reassuring words. God's thoughts towards me are wonderful. Allow this verse to minister to your heart. Allow the Lord to change the way you think about yourself to see yourself the way He sees your life which He says is peaceful, and hopeful. From this day forth, we will not listen to the lies of the enemy. We will cast down all vain imaginations that try to acknowledge itself above the knowledge of God and bring every thought into captivity to the obedience of Christ. What negative thoughts are you thinking about yourself, about your life? In order to have positive thinking, we must daily confess the word of God over our lives. Confess positive confessions because you are a new creation in Christ Jesus.

Let Us Pray

Our Heavenly Father;

I ask that You transform my mind and make it like You. In Jesus name, I pray.

Amen.

REFLECTION

_____

_____

_____

_____

_____

_____

_____

_____

_____

_____

_____

_____

_____

_____

_____

_____

REFLECTION

Day 10 GOD, MY HELP WITH SICKNESS

O Lord my God, I cried out to You, and you healed me.
–PSALM 30:2

*For I will restore health to you and
heal you of your wounds, says the Lord.*
–JEREMIAH 30:17

Devotion

Healing is available to God's children. God is saying cry out to Me, pray to Me. I will heal you of your sickness. I will restore any broken bones; all health challenges you face. I am here to restore you. With what are you plagued? Is it diabetes, high blood pressure, lupus, overweight, back issues, infertility, a broken bone, cancer or kidney diseases?

Today, I challenge you. Whose report will you believe? I encourage you to believe God's report. Claim your healing. God did not come that we should die in sickness! He took sickness captive and when He rose from the grave He won the victory over all sickness, manner of disease, and health concerns. Speak the word over your life, your love ones, and watch God turn the situation around. He can do it if we only believe. It is hard sometimes when things are not looking hopeful and you're scared because you don't know the outcome. In those moments, trust God with His word. Trust God that His perfect will, will be done. He knows what is best for us. Walk by faith, and not by sight. God is here. He is the God who heals. Healing is the will of God.

Let Us Pray

Our Heavenly Father;

I stand upon Your word and claim my healing. Thank You for this blessed hope that You are restoring me back to you. In Jesus name, I pray.

Amen.

REFLECTION

REFLECTION

_____

_____

_____

_____

_____

_____

_____

_____

_____

_____

_____

_____

_____

_____

Day 11 GOD, MY HELP WITH DECISIONS

Be anxious for nothing, but in everything by prayer and supplication, with thanksgiving, let your requests be made known to God; and the peace of God, which surpasses all understanding, will guard your hearts and minds through Christ Jesus.

–PHILIPPIANS 4:6-7

Devotion

The word "decision" is defined as a conclusion or resolution reached after consideration. We make decisions on a daily basis. What am I going to wear to work? What route am I going to drive to work? What toothpaste to purchase from the pharmacy? These types of decisions are often easy to make. But what about the big decisions like, "What school am I going to enroll my child? Should I pursue this relationship? Should I take the job offer? Is this the right person to marry?" Whether the decision is simple or complex, how many of us involve God in the decision making process. I am sure some decisions require a lot more thought than others. Here are some points to consider when making decisions.

1. *Stop and Pray* – Philippians 4: 6-7 teaches us that we should not be so quick to make a decision. We should give careful consideration through prayer. The reason for that is whatever decision made, if we are guided by the Holy Spirit, He promises to bring peace. Peace which will surpass a level of your comprehension that you will say, "Only for the grace of God."

2. *Seek Counsel* – Do not be foolish when making a decision. Proverbs 11: 14 says where there is not counsel, the people fall; but in the multitude of counselors, there is safety. Ask the hard questions when making decisions. Weigh the pros and cons. Seek out Christian individuals who have experienced similar circumstances to help. This encourages, and strengthen, your decision and often times help you not to make a big mistake.

3. *Acquire wisdom* – James 1: 5 reads, "If any of you lacks wisdom, let him ask of God, who gives to all liberally and without reproach, and it will be given to him." Wisdom is the action step taken based upon the level of understanding obtained from factual knowledge bringing about a positive result. You wonder why you keep getting the same results, it is your lack of wisdom.

The Holy Spirit is here to help us today to make the right decisions. Simply put, God knows what is best for us. Seek his face and watch your plans prosper.

Let Us Pray

Our Heavenly Father;

I submit to You today that your ways are perfect and best for my life. Guide me in truth with my decisions I need to make today. I incline my ear and heart to You. In Jesus name, I pray.

Amen.

REFLECTION

_____

_____

_____

_____

_____

_____

_____

_____

_____

_____

_____

_____

_____

_____

_____

_____

REFLECTION

Day 12 GOD, MY HELP WITH FORGIVENESS

For if you forgive men their trespasses, your heavenly Father will also forgive you. But if you do not forgive men their trespasses, neither will your Father forgive your trespasses.

–MATTHEW 6:14-15

Devotion

Forgiveness is the action or process of forgiving or being forgiven. It is a conscious, deliberate decision to release feelings of hurt, anger, resentment, bitterness, or vengeance towards a person who harmed you either physically, emotionally, psychologically or even financially. Forgiveness doesn't mean forgetting nor does it mean condoning the action or behavior. Forgiveness allows you to heal and to see the person how God sees them. Also to realize that God has forgiven you when you messed up and we have no right to cast judgment on anyone. Allow God to deal with the situation. The bible shows us when you forgive it provides four blessings of hope and peace.

1. When you forgive, God forgives you. Don't hold a grudge (Matthew 6: 14)

2. When you forgive, God hears and answers your prayers (Mark 11: 25)

3. When you forgive, God will grant you mercy and favor with man in times of need (Matthew 18: 21-27)

4. When you forgive, God's unconditional love continues to be manifested in your daily life and our hearts develop into His image and likeness (Romans 5: 8)

Today, don't allow unforgiveness to rule in your heart. Be kind and be merciful. It gives you a level of peace and matures you in Christ Jesus.

Let Us Pray

Our Heavenly Father;

Today, I forgive _____ for what they did to me. I thank You for removing this heavy burden off of me. I now walk in peace and love. In Jesus name, I pray.

Amen.

REFLECTION

REFLECTION

_____

_____

_____

_____

_____

_____

_____

_____

_____

_____

_____

_____

_____

_____

_____

_____

Day 13
GOD, MY HELP WITH RESTING

I will both lie down in peace, and sleep;
For you alone, O Lord, make me dwell in safety.
–PSALM 4:8

Devotion

Rest is so important to the body. It is said that individuals should get at least 7 to 9 hours sleep to function at their best on a daily basis. Do you get 8 hours sleep on a regular basis or are you only getting 5 to 6 hours? What is it that is keeping you from getting the hours needed for proper brain functionality and body health? Do you know adequate rest allows your muscles, nerves, bones, and connective tissue time to rebuild from the previous days' activity? In our day to day lives, we have so much going on that we find ourselves losing out on sleep. Whether it is checking late night homework, washing a load of laundry, money problems, death, completing an assignment, and thinking about situations that may be burdensome and worry us, our body needs rest. In spite of it all,

God promised in His word to give us sweet sleep. Rest is an opportunity for:

1. God to speak to us in visions and dreams concerning situations in our lives (Job 33: 15)

2. To heal us, when we are sick (John 11: 12)

3. Give you peace, comfort and protection (Proverbs 3: 24)

4. Your mind and heart becomes at ease (Matthew 11: 28-30)

Embrace sleep today. Ask the Lord to take control of your sleep, to refresh you so you can think more clearly each day.

Let Us Pray

Our Heavenly Father;

Thank you for your promise. This day, I welcome you into my quiet space and I ask that you give me a sweet and peaceful sleep. Speak to me as I sleep giving me clear direction for the new day. In Jesus name, I pray.

Amen.

REFLECTION

REFLECTION

_____

_____

_____

_____

_____

_____

_____

_____

_____

_____

_____

_____

_____

_____

_____

_____

Day 14 GOD, MY HELP WITH MARRIAGE

For this reason a man shall leave his father and mother and
be joined to his wife, and the two shall become one flesh.
So then, they are no longer two but one flesh. Therefore,
what God has joined together, let not man separate.

–MATTHEW 19:5-6

Devotion

Marriage is a beautiful and wonderful gift from God. An institution created by God that He has ordained from the beginning of time as honorable. NO two people are alike and no two people are perfect. But the good news is marriage is perfect. Because God is perfect. With this in mind, it simply tells us that God must be the foundation of a marriage. God is the one that has to breathe on your marriage daily for it to become the full manifestation and reflection of the kingdom of God. It is not in my spouse changing that cause my marriage to change or if I become this perfect individual my marriage will change. This is all lies. What is truth? God sees and He knows what is best for your marriage! He said in Matthew in our devotional scripture today that the two shall become one flesh and what God has joined let no one separate. It is important to get in prayer and in the word of God to gain understanding and guidance for your marriage. You cannot become one if you haven't submitted your marriage to God. God joined you both together so only He can keep you together. Humans are fickle individuals. One day we are in love and the next day we are out of love because of something our spouse has done. Today, ask God to show you, to mold you both, to fuse you both together as one, and to allow flesh to die and the spirit to live in your marriage. As you do this, God will guide you on what is lacking and needed in your marriage for it to grow and blossom. Fight for your marriage. God wants it to succeed.

Let Us Pray

Our Heavenly Father;

Today, I need you to cover my marriage in Your blood. Saturate it with what it needs. Forgive me for taking my marriage for granted. I ask that You teach me on what I need to do for my marriage to succeed. I resist the devil. He has no authority in my marriage. You, God, are in control. In Jesus name, I pray.

Amen.

REFLECTION

REFLECTION

_____

_____

_____

_____

_____

_____

_____

_____

_____

_____

_____

_____

_____

_____

_____

_____

Day 15

GOD, MY HELP WITH TIME MANAGEMENT

So teach us to number our days, that we may gain a heart of wisdom.

–PSALM 90:12

Devotion

There are 24 Hours in a day and 365 days in a year. What are you doing with your time? Are you using it wisely? Psalm 90 speaks about the importance of time management. It is showing us that life is short when not focused and purpose driven. God wants us to be intentional about how we use our time. We need to ask God to teach us how to manage each day He gives to us. As He teaches us, we will gain the wisdom on our day to day activities resulting in a productive day. Ecclesiastes 3 says there is a time for everything under the sun. Which means, time is always moving. It can never be regained. There is a time to be born and a time to die. What is important to God is the in-between. What are we doing with the time God gives us? Our life is meant to be purposeful. We are here to bring solution to a problem. Ask God to help you identify your purpose. When you understand your purpose, your 24 hours and

365 days become precious - not to be wasted on activities which bring no gain, no peace, no joy, and no contentment. I admonish you today; trust the Heavenly Father with your day. Commit it to Him and watch Him establish your ways.

Let Us Pray

Our Heavenly Father;

I ask that You teach me how to manage each day. As I submit to your purpose and plan for my life, wisdom will shine on my day. In Jesus name, I pray.

Amen.

REFLECTION

_____

_____

_____

_____

_____

_____

_____

_____

_____

_____

_____

_____

_____

_____

_____

REFLECTION

_____

_____

_____

_____

_____

_____

_____

_____

_____

_____

_____

_____

_____

_____

_____

_____

Day 16
GOD, MY HELP WITH OBEDIENCE

But he said, "More than that, blessed are those
who hear the word of God and keep it."

–LUKE 11:28

Devotion

Obedience is defined as compliance with an order, request, or law to another's authority. Throughout the Bible, we see where God gives instructions to His people to follow. Some obeyed immediately and others disobeyed and experience negative consequences. God's intention for humanity from the beginning of time was to walk in total obedience. Obedience to God shows our love towards Him. His love towards us was creating us to obey Him but because of sin, we fell out of true fellowship with Him. As a result, humanity's desire to walk in obedience is challenged daily. What is the Lord asking you to do specifically? May I encourage you to follow the instructions of the Lord? Obey his voice today. It may not look like it makes sense, but trust God. He knows the beginning from the end. Move in faith and watch the Lord see you through. Be encouraged with Deuteronomy 31: 8 (New Living Translation) which says, "Do not be afraid or discouraged, for the Lord will personally go ahead of you."

Let Us Pray

Our Heavenly Father;

I give You my life. Use me for Your glory. I surrender my will and accept Your will for my life. Here I am send me. In Jesus name, I pray.

Amen.

REFLECTION**)**

REFLECTION

_____

_____

_____

_____

_____

_____

_____

_____

_____

_____

_____

_____

_____

_____

_____

_____

Day 17
GOD, MY HELP WITH MONEY

But seek first the kingdom of God and His righteousness, and all these things shall be added to you. Therefore do not worry about tomorrow, for tomorrow will worry about its own things. Sufficient for the day is its own trouble.

–MATTHEW 6:33-34

Honor the Lord with your possessions.

–PROVERBS 3:9

Devotion

Finances are critical to an individual's life. School fees, house mortgage, rent, gas, grocery, light bill, water bill, medical bills, tithes, offering, loans, saving; the list could go on. Every day we need money for something. Do you ever open your wallet and say how am I going to do this today? Or looked at your pay check and frowned because you knew deep down those digits are not enough to cover the list of expenses you currently have? In our devotion today, God speaks to His children directly and say do not worry. I know what you need before you ask. But I need you to seek Me first. Put Me first. When you seek Me and put Me first, you will find Me and I will supply all your needs. God knows how much you need to run your household. But how many of us honor the Lord first with the blessings he has given us? I mean hold up the pay check and thank God for giving you the ability to work and so you are now receiving financial resources from the use of your gift. This is important. God bless you, so allow God to take care of you. You can't do it on your own. You need wisdom on how to operate your finances. Only God can give you the wisdom on how to maximize your pay check. Ecclesiastes 7: 12 says "for wisdom is a defense, as money is a defense. But the excellence of knowledge is that wisdom give life to those who have it". You don't have a money problem. You have a wisdom problem! Put God to a test today. Spend time in prayer and present the pay check to God and watch Him give you the wisdom and tools on how to budget out every dollar and cent and give you extra. God is loving and faithful. Trust Him to help you today.

Let Us Pray

Our Heavenly Father;

Today, I present to you my finances. You see and know what is best for me and my family. I cannot do this on my own. Teach me today how to manage my money. I want to honor You with my possessions. In Jesus name, I pray.

Amen.

REFLECTION

REFLECTION

Day 18
GOD, MY HELP WITH GRIEF

Blessed be the God and Father of our Lord Jesus Christ, the Father of mercies and God of all comfort, who comforts us in all our tribulation, that we may be able to comfort those who are in any trouble, with the comfort with which we ourselves are comforted by God.

–2 CORINTHIANS 1:3-4

Devotion

I'm trusting in You, Lord. I'm trusting in You. When I look at the situation Lord, all I can do, I'm trusting in You, Lord. I'm trusting in You. At some point in our lives, we will experience the loss of a love one. It is not easy to lose someone so near and dear to your heart. It is difficult to pick up the pieces and move on with life. You feel hopeless, alone, like the world has sucked the very breath out of your body. Why did my love one have to die? Couldn't I have more time with them? How am I going to move on from day to day? Today, God is saying, He is your burden bearer. He is here to comfort you, and to heal your broken heart. Only He understands and knows what is going on inside of you. During grief, it is important to do the following until you gain a sense of normalcy.

1. Visit the grave for closure

2. View family photos to remember the happy moments of your love one

3. Journal to express the pain of the loss

4. Take an artistic class for example poetry, painting or drawing. This activity actually releases negative energy in the body

5. Eat at least once a day to maintain your nourishment, grief can sometime take your appetite

6. Speak with a grief counselor if you feel yourself slipping into a deep depression or join a support group

7. Get a prayer partner who will pray with you and with whom you can converse

8. Cry! Crying begins the grieving process and opens the door to healing.

God is with you. He feels every pain. Trust today that He will renew your strength.

Let Us Pray

Our Heavenly Father;

I am in a lot of pain. I don't know how to live day to day. I need You to wrap Your loving arms around me today and comfort me. My heart aches to see _____ again but I know they are in a better place. Please remember me and renew my strength. In Jesus name, I pray.

Amen.

REFLECTION

REFLECTION

Day 19

GOD, MY HELP WITH HEARING

Your ears shall hear a word behind you saying,
"this is the way, walk in it," whenever you turn to the right hand
or whenever you turn to the left.

–ISAIAH 30:21

Devotion

Hearing God's voice is as precious as a crying baby being comforted by its mother. The baby believes that his/her mother can only sooth. God's voice provides so much safety, peace, and direction in our everyday life. When things seem confusing, just one word from God will help to ease the circumstances. God encourages us throughout His word to continuously seek Him, and when we seek Him, we will find Him. When we find Him, He will speak and begin to reveal the answers we need. Hearing God's voice is a life line. We, his children, should daily hunger to hear His voice. He says in John 10: 27, "My sheep hear my voice, and I know them, and they follow me." We are the sheep of God's pasture. He longs to lead us daily. We must position ourselves daily to hear when God speaks. The more we spend time in prayer, reading a verse daily, and following the words of the Bible, our hearts and our minds are transformed and renewed. When this happens, our spirit man comes alive and connects with the Holy Spirit who will lead us into truth. John 6: 63 confirms this by saying, "it is the spirit who gives life; the flesh is no help at all. The words that I have spoken to you are spirit and life." What is it that you need God's direction on? Jeremiah 33: 3 says, "Call to me and I will answer you and will tell you great and hidden things that you have not known." We have to intentionally kill our flesh daily and command our spirit man which resides on the inside to come alive so that you can commune with your Heavenly Father. It will not happen with not doing anything. We must maintain a discipline life. Start off small, one verse a week and daily read it. Speak it out loud and confess it over your life. The more of the word you have, and the understanding, and putting it into practice, you begin to hear God's voice, clearer because your faith is growing. I close with this scripture Romans 10: 17, "So then faith comes from hearing, and hearing by the word of God."

Let Us Pray

Our Heavenly Father;

I incline my ears to Your voice. I block out my voice and the voices around me. I only want to hear Your voice and follow Your instructions. Today, I declare that I am submitted to You. In Jesus name, I pray.

Amen.

REFLECTION

_____

_____

_____

_____

_____

_____

_____

_____

_____

_____

_____

_____

_____

_____

_____

REFLECTION

_____

_____

_____

_____

_____

_____

_____

_____

_____

_____

_____

_____

_____

_____

_____

_____

Day 20 GOD, MY HELP WITH DISCIPLINE

My flesh and my heart fail,
but God is the strength of my heart and my portion forever.

–PSALM 73:26

Devotion

Having a devoted life to God, provides you with a life filled with peace, joy, love, security and hope. Though the winds may blow and storms may come leaving you to wonder, God is right there to give you strength to continue pressing on from day to day. Romans 14: 8 reminds us that in life and death we are the Lord's. This was God's plans for His creation from day one. We all have a great reward if we hold to the faith. Devotion is commitment and loyalty to a person. Jesus loves us very much and is always devoted to us that while we were sinners He died for us. We weren't deserving but yet He calls us His children. Shouldn't we give Him the same level of devotion with our time, our talent and our treasure? God is calling us today. Calling us to a place in Him that will provide rest and comfort for your soul? If you need that today, stop what you are doing and make God a priority. He is waiting.

Let Us Pray

Our Heavenly Father;

You are the source of my strength. I give You my life today. In Jesus name, I pray.

Amen.

REFLECTION

_____

_____

_____

_____

_____

_____

_____

_____

_____

_____

_____

_____

_____

_____

_____

_____

REFLECTION

_____

_____

_____

_____

_____

_____

_____

_____

_____

_____

_____

_____

_____

_____

_____

Day 21
GOD, MY HELP WITH SELF PERCEPTION

I will praise You, for I am fearfully and wonderfully made;
Marvelous are Your works and that my soul knows very well.

–PSALM 139:14

Devotion

You are not a mistake. You are not unusual. You are not the child to get the handouts or the black sheep in the family. YOU ARE NOT! Why do you allow these thoughts to flood your mind on a daily basis? Do you not know you are the apple of God's eye? A jewel in His hand. His friend. His daughter. The head and not the tail, above and not beneath. You are fearfully and wonderfully made by God, formed in your mother's womb to be someone in this world. Don't listen to the lies of the enemy anymore. God has a beautiful plan for our lives and He made you just the way you are in order to complete the assignment He has called you to fulfill. Embrace your uniqueness. Embrace your looks, your shape, your personality, and your character. It is all in the Master's plan. The world is waiting on you to shine. Someone is looking for your lighthouse to be guided to safety. Romans 8:1-2 gives us hope reminding us there is no condemnation to those in Christ Jesus. You have God's DNA so walk in faith, and boldness. Of course, people are not going to like you, and that is fine. Be different! It is a gift from God. You were born to standout.

Let Us Pray

Our Heavenly Father;

I declare over my life I am who You say I am. I can do all things through Christ who gives me strength. In Jesus name, I pray.

Amen.

REFLECTION

REFLECTION

_____

_____

_____

_____

_____

_____

_____

_____

_____

_____

_____

_____

_____

_____

_____

Prayers of Change

Father, in the name of Jesus, I decree and declare;

1. Oh, how I love you.

2. This is the day that you have made. I will rejoice. I am extremely glad. My soul makes a boast in you Lord.

3. I arise to proclaim, You are God and besides You, there is none other.

4. You are Father, my daddy, my help, my king, my joy, my peace, my protector, my provider, my love, the sustainer of my mind, the Lilly of the valley, the bright and morning star, Yahweh, and the lion of the tribe of Judah. Praise be unto You, Jehovah God.

5. I plead the blood that was shed for me, over me now. Trouble the waters now and remove the guilt, the shame, the pain, the hurt, the disgust, the stigma, the sin from off of my life. Forgive me. Help me to see myself the way You see me.

6. I pull down every strong hold around me - my family, my job, my church, and everything that is connected to me. Breathe your Shekinah Glory upon my environment now.

7. Everything that is designed to live, I command to live. Everything that is designed to die, let it be so in Jesus name. I represent You God as I leave this home. Use me for Your glory.

8. I am made in your image and in your likeness. All things pertaining to life and godliness are mine today.

9. My head is anointed with oil today. I have the mind of Christ. I think on those things that are just, of a good report, lovely and praiseworthy. I forget those things that are behind, and I reach towards those things that are in front of me. I pull down every vain imagination that tries to exalt itself against the knowledge of God. I am not of this world. I am transformed by the renewing of my mind. Behold, old things have passed away. Behold, all things are now new. Now, it is springing forth in my life.

10. Today, I am not walking in the counsel of the ungodly. I will not sit down where the scornful gather. I delight myself in the Lord for Him to fulfill the purpose and plan He has set out for my life. I am not tossed to and from by any wind or false doctrine. So, today I will study Your word to show myself approved. I will not be brought to shame or ashamed of who's I am. Your word is teaching me today how to live right.

11. I give my body to You. This body is the temple in which You dwell. I will not defile it. I now command that:

    a. My eyes see You clearly.

    b. My mouth speak life and not death and to speak when You direct me to speak. I will stay away from idle gossip.

c. My ears to hear Your voice and be obedient.

d. My hands to always be filled with provision to bring You glory in the earth.

e. My feet to go only where You need me to go.

12. I am all God calls me to be because He said in Psalm 139: 14, "I am fearfully and wonderfully made."

13. I will trust in the Lord with all my heart and lean not to my own understanding, but in all my ways I will acknowledge You and You will direct my path today (Proverbs 3: 5-6).

14. I have the victory today. Victory in my mind. Victory in my body. Victory in my spirit because God said He was wounded, and bruised for me on the cross at Calvary and when He died, He got the keys from hell and so Satan has no power over me.

15. I will bless the Lord at all times. Today, I will bless Him with my actions, my thoughts, and my words (Psalms 34: 1).

16. I am free from the bondages of sin as I purpose in myself to live a life of holiness and righteousness unto God.

17. My desires are Jesus desires and as I seek after Him; His glory will not only be upon me but in me and seen through me.

18. I will be a submissive, supportive, understanding, and a prayerful woman, wife, mother, employee, employer, and church member.

19. I am controlled by the Holy Spirit.

20. I am seeking after those things which gratify the Holy Spirit which is living a life of love, joy, peace, patience, kindness, goodness, faithfulness, gentleness, and self-control (Galatians 5: 22).

21. In this season of my life, I will not speak my way out of my promise. AMEN.

About the Author
CHRISTINA MOSELEY ROLLE

Beach lover, avid reader, leader, mother and wife, Christina Moseley – Rolle enjoys *"minding her own business."*

Christina has been employed in the Culinary Arts & Tourism Studies Unit at The University of Bahamas since 2006. Moseley-Rolle earned a Master of Science degree in Organizational Learning and Leadership from Barry University; a Bachelor of Science in Hotel Management from the University of West Indies and an associate's in Culinary Arts from the Bahamas Hotel Training College.

In 2007, she became the first beneficiary of the Faculty Exchange Program between The University of The Bahamas and Monroe College in New Rochelle, NY where she served as a pastry chef instructor during the summer session from April to August.

Throughout her career, Christina completed certifications and training in Human Resource Management, Supervisory & Administrative Skills, Effective Writing Skills, Leadership and Disaster Preparedness. She also obtained training through the John

Maxwell Leadership Training Course and the Johnson & Wales Culinary Essentials Educators Program in Miami, Florida.

She has over 18 years of experience in the hospitality industry and has held various positions in her family-owned business, Original Patties Bakery, Limited in Nassau, Bahamas.

Christina is constantly evolving and growing the membership at her church - *New Destiny Fellowship Center*. In her role as the director of the women's ministry at NDFC, she has organized various activities including monthly bible study meetings, the annual Ignite the Fire Women's Conference and the Lady in Red Valentine's Dinner.

Christina is married to Bishop-Elect Nathan Rolle. They are blessed with three wonderful children: Devon, Alyanna and Abigail. For self-care, you can find her on the beach reflecting on her goals, watching 80s and 90s sitcoms and spending time with her loved ones.

Christina's future literary projects and expansion will focus on refreshing family structure through a 12-week mentorship program and retreats for women from all walks of life.

Christina is available to speak and teach at conferences, international women's events on prayer and leadership. You can email her team at christinamoseleyrolle@outlook.com

As you finish this journal, please connect and tag Christina on Facebook @christinamoseleyrolle. Also, email your testimony to christinamoseleyrolle@outlook.com. We just might feature you on our website, christinarolle.com!

www.ingramcontent.com/pod-product-compliance
Lightning Source LLC
Chambersburg PA
CBHW070053100426
42740CB00013B/2835